The Ship in the Fog

By Sally Cowan

T0342853

Shan and Bill had lots of clams to sell at the shop.

The clams were in shells.

Bill shut the lid on a big box of clam shells.

Shan's ship was then in a big fog.

This fog is bad!
Let's get this ship to the shed.

Shan's ship got tossed up.

"I can not see the cliffs," yelled Bill.
"The ship will hit them!"

"Let's get the tug man
on the phone!" said Shan.

Shan had a chat with
the tug man.

Then, Shan's ship went into a gap in the fog.

"Look!" yelled Bill.
"We will hit the cliffs!"

But the tug got to Shan's ship.

It did **not** hit the cliffs!

The tug got the ship
to its shed.

CHECKING FOR MEANING

1. What was in the big box? *(Literal)*

2. Why couldn't Bill see the cliffs? *(Literal)*

3. How did the tug help Shan and Bill's ship? *(Inferential)*

EXTENDING VOCABULARY

clams	What are *clams*? Why do people buy clams at a shop? What do clams taste like? Are they salty? Slippery? Creamy?
ship	What are other words that mean the same as *ship*? What are the names of some different types of ships or boats? E.g. canoe, dinghy, trawler, cruiser.
phone	What sound does the digraph *ph–* make in this word? *Phone* is the short form of a longer word. What is the longer word?

MOVING BEYOND THE TEXT

1. Why were Shan and Bill out on the ship?
   What work do they do?

2. What types of seafood can you name? What is your favourite? Why?

3. Why is fog dangerous for ships? What might have happened to Shan and Bill in the fog?

4. Why are tug boats helpful for larger ships?
   Where could you see a tug boat at work?

SPEED SOUNDS

sh	ch	th	th	wh	qu	ph
		voiced	unvoiced			

Shan

shop

shells

shut

ship

then

this

shed

them

chat

Then

Shan's

This